Scenes for Teens

50 Original Comedy and Drama Scenes for Teenage Actors

Mike Kimmel

Foreword by Kevin Sorbo

ISBN-10: 1497557038
ISBN-13: 9781497557031
Library of Congress Control Number: 2014906650
CreateSpace Independent Publishing Platform
North Charleston, South Carolina

Praise for *Scenes for Teens*

"Mike Kimmel's scenes for young actors are perfect for young talent just starting out. These scenes give young people situations they can relate to and the ability to make some real choices, while learning some valuable life lessons at the same time. I also like the pace these scenes set. They are conversational and real."
  - Ryan Glorioso
  Glorioso Casting

"Well done, Mike! These teen scenes are funny, touching, accessible and great teaching tools not only for acting but for life."
  - Emily Mann
  Artistic Director & Resident Playwright,
  McCarter Theatre Center
  National Theatre Conference Person of the Year, 2011

"*Scenes for Teens* is a must have for young artists who are serious about honing their craft. Mike has used his writing talents to put together a collection of scenes with varying dialogue styles that is invaluable in assisting young actors in working with different writers when moving from one project to the next."
  - George Landrum Jr.
  Landrum Arts LA Talent Agency

"*Scenes for Teens* is a great resource for teen actors. It is a must have tool for any teenager wanting to pursue an acting career."
  - Lisa Marie Dupree
  Casting Director, Films In Motion

"This is a wonderful collection that teens will find very helpful in their auditions. Good job, Mike Kimmel!"
- Debi Derryberry
Actor & Voice-Over Artist, *Jimmy Neutron, Family Guy, Toy Story, Toy Story 2, iCarly, The Lorax, Curious George*

"This is great material for beginning teen actors. It is evident that Mike genuinely cares for his students and the potential of their young careers."
- Dana Gourrier
Actor, *Django Unchained, Lee Daniels's The Butler, Treme, American Horror Story, True Detectives*

"Even an aspiring stunt performer should pick this up, because it pays to deliver your lines eloquently before getting thrown off a building."
- Gene LeBell
Legendary Stuntman, *Raging Bull, Man on the Moon, L.A. Confidential, Spiderman 2, Batman & Robin, Rocky IV, Any Which Way You Can, The Fall Guy, The Munsters*

"Mike Kimmel has been around the show biz game for a long time. He's been on both sides of the camera and has a great deal of knowledge to share with young performers. Buy this book!"
- Johnny Valiant
Professional Wrestler, WWE Hall of Fame
Three-Time World Tag Team Champion

For Mollie, Adele, and Tammy,
my three beautiful sisters.

"The very best thing you can do for the whole world is to make the most of yourself."

- Wallace Wattles

Table of Contents

Foreword

Everyone knows the old stereotypes about show business. It's tough. There are no guarantees of success. The best actor doesn't always get the part. Some of the most skilled performers are waiting tables and driving taxis.

Despite these brutal realities, actors continue to line up for the chance to perform on stage and screen. I applaud teenagers who have the courage to pursue careers in show biz. I love working with talented young people. I get inspired and renewed by their energy and enthusiasm. I've always felt that experienced actors have a responsibility to give something back by mentoring newcomers, and lending a helping hand to the next generation.

I've had great opportunities, and have been privileged to enjoy wonderful success in the entertainment industry. It wasn't easy. Nothing about it was easy. It took a ton of work. Before I won the role of Hercules, I pounded the pavement hard in Hollywood. I took acting classes twice a week, and chased down every audition opportunity I could. I worked in commercials and modeling, networked with other actors, and built relationships with casting directors, agents, managers, directors, and producers.

I believe that discipline is the most valuable quality young actors can develop. Without the discipline I learned from years of playing competitive sports, and trudging through the harsh Minnesota winters of my youth, I don't know if I could have kept going through the difficult times. And believe me, there were plenty of difficult times.

Discipline is the great equalizer. Discipline will keep you moving forward when it looks like nobody in the world believes in you. As tough as this industry is, try to remember that newcomers are cast in their very first projects each and every day.

Discipline yourself to work harder, longer, and more creatively than you think you can. The secret of success is always hard work. There are never any short cuts. Take the time to study, learn, rehearse, and perform the scenes in this book. The process will do you a world of good.

Every audition is a new job interview, and even the best actors have to prove themselves over and over again. Never, ever, give up on yourself. I've been where you are today, and I wish you all the very best of happiness and success.

Kevin Sorbo
Los Angeles, California

Acknowledgments

Many thanks to my wonderful friends, Kimberley Bliquez, GiGi Erneta, Sharon Garrison, Nancy Chartier, Chuck Disney, and David Breland. Your support and encouragement have been invaluable and are greatly appreciated.

Special thanks to Kevin Sorbo, a true hero on screen and off, for believing in this project from the very beginning.

Introduction

It's not fair. Being an actor is tough enough, but teenagers have it even tougher.

Although teenage actors need to develop the same skill set as their adult counterparts, they have an additional challenge to overcome.

Think about it. Teenagers usually play supporting characters in television, film, and theater. There are exceptions to this, of course, but teen roles are generally secondary to the older characters, who play the leads in most scripts.

Teenage roles, then, tend to be shorter than those written for adults. Unfortunately, many are also cluttered up with props, multiple entrances and exits, and additional supporting cast members. Even teen scenes from popular movies, television shows, and plays are often too short and filled with too many distractions to be effective teaching tools. Because of this, it's hard to find good material to replicate audition scenarios and train young actors to deliver their lines in a real and conversational style.

Through consistent practice with two-person scenes, actors can develop active listening and naturalistic speaking skills. Listening intently is just as important as speaking, and is often overlooked when coaching beginners. Active listening "draws people in" and encourages them to pay attention to the actor's *silent reactions* to dialogue. Scenes performed in this way more closely resemble real conversations.

It must always look like the actor is having a real conversation with another person. That's where the expression "it has to be real" comes from in show business. If it's real, then the audience can enjoy what's called "a willing suspension of disbelief." That means people can escape reality for a while and convince themselves that the actors are creating the action as it unfolds on stage or screen. The most effective way to develop these skills is to work with scenes that are free of props, special costuming requirements, and other background noise, allowing actors to focus on the one-on-one relationship.

That's the reason behind *Scenes for Teens*. I've been blessed to work, audition, and teach in the two largest markets in the country, Los Angeles and New York, as well as expanding regional areas. All markets have something in common: agents, casting directors, producers, and directors that are open and receptive to well-trained young talent. Acting teachers and private coaches, however, struggle to find appropriate material to prepare teenagers to book professional projects.

Scenes for Teens is meant to help fill this need. The scenes are written for two actors, are gender-neutral, and avoid extraneous characters, props, costumes, entrances, and exits. In this way, *Scenes for Teens* is specifically designed to help young actors practice dialogue in a conversational, realistic manner.

That's why the characters in *Scenes for Teens* are just called "A and B," rather than given specific male and female names. A wonderful exercise used by experienced actors is to switch roles with their scene partners. Naming characters "A and B" makes swapping roles simpler, more natural, and much less daunting. This training also helps actors become familiar and comfortable with improvisation.

Thank you for selecting this book. I'd like to see young actors practice and perform these scenes so realistically that anyone watching will believe you're having actual conversations with your best friends. I sincerely hope teenagers will benefit from the positive messages and life lessons included here, as well.

I believe in you. Now go get 'em.

Mike Kimmel
New Orleans, Louisiana

Comedy Scenes

Got a Light?

A Do you have a cigarette?

B No.

A No?

B No. I don't smoke.

A I thought you smoked.

B No. Never. I've never smoked a cigarette in my life.

A I've *seen* you smoke.

B You have *never* seen me smoke. I've never smoked a single cigarette in my entire life.

A Why not?

B I hate cigarettes, and I can't stand being around second-hand smoke.

A Why?

B Why? It's gross and disgusting!

A Why are you so negative?

B Because cigarettes are disgusting! Why do you even smoke?!

A I don't know. I like it. It's cool.

B What's cool about it?

A It's relaxing. It's cool. Everybody smokes.

B *Everybody* smokes?

A Yeah. Everybody I know. All the cool people. Everybody that's cool at school smokes. That's what people do.

B You're not giving me very good reasons.

A It's very *social*. People go outside and take cigarette breaks *together*.

B Cigarettes make your teeth yellow and make your breath smell like feet.

A You'd get along better with people if you smoked. It's very social.

B Skanky, nasty, disgusting, smelly feet.

A Smoking is good for when you want to take a break. You know, a coffee break, a cigarette break. It's just nice. I could quit anytime I feel like it.

B So why don't you?

A I don't feel like it.

B Okay. Aren't they kind of expensive?

A Yeah. Kinda.

B Where do you get the money?

A Uh…all around. My folks.

B Your parents give you money for cigarettes?

A No. I…uh… take it. They don't know. Sometimes I just take it.

B Wow.

A Don't look at me like that.

B Like what?

A Like you're judging me.

B I'm not judging anybody.

A You look like you're judging me.

B Nope.

A That's what it looks like.

B Feet.

A What?

B Skanky, nasty, disgusting, smelly feet.

A You are being so rude today. I can't believe you.

B *Expensive,* skanky, nasty, disgusting, smelly feet.

Can I Borrow a Pencil?

A Can I borrow a pencil?

B What kind?

A The kind you write on sheets of paper with.

B No! I mean what kind of pencil do you want? What hardness? What variety?

A I don't know. Something that writes, has a sharp point, and still has enough eraser left over that I can fix something if I make a mistake.

B Are you taking an exam?

A Why do you ask that question?

B If you have a standardized test, you'll need a number 2 pencil.

A Oh! I get it now!

B Yeah. A number 2 pencil has exactly the right amount of graphite to be picked up by the Scantron.

A Scantron?

B The machine they use to grade papers.

A Oh, right, right, right...

B Yeah.

A No, I don't have any tests.

B Good.

A Except now I'm starting to feel like....uh...

B Yeah?

A Like I'm being tested by you.

B Hey, I'm just trying to help.

A Okay.

B I'm just trying to explain all the different varieties of pencils so you'll be familiar with them and can make good choices.

A Okay. Now I'm familiar with them and I'm confident I can make good choices.

B Well, I think that's great. Great. Not just good, but great. Really great.

A Thank you.

B You're welcome.

A As a matter of fact, if I had something to write with, I'd take notes on all this stuff. All this not just good, but great, really great information.

B Well, I think that'd be a smart move.

A Thank you.

B You're welcome.

A So can I?

B Can you what?

A Borrow a stupid pencil!

B Oh, I don't have any. I don't like to write with pencils.

A Great. Just great. Not just good, but great. Really great.

B Thank you.

A You're welcome.

B Thank you for saying "You're welcome."

A You're welcome.

Driver's Ed

A Are you taking Driver's Ed next semester?

B No, my mom is teaching me to drive instead.

A Cool. Your mom is awesome.

B Yeah, we had our first lesson a couple of days ago. I think it's going to work out great.

A Is she a good teacher?

B I think so. She's very patient with me.

A That's really important.

B She's a really good driver too. She hardly ever hits anything.

A That's great. She's probably really careful.

B So far so good.

A My mom runs over stuff all the time. She should take Driver's Ed with me.

B Maybe she has to get driving glasses just because she's getting older.

A No. She just gets distracted. She's always on the phone, drinking coffee, and putting on make-up.

B That's bad.

A Real bad. The phone is one thing, but putting on make-up is ridiculous.

B Good thing she's not teaching you to drive.

A That's why I'm taking Driver's Ed.

B   Does she text?

A   No!! We never showed her how!!

B   Good thinking.

A   Tell me about it.

B   I just did.

Driver's Ed is Good
For Your Head

A Hey! What's up?

B Not much. How's the driving lessons with your mom going?

A So far so good.

B No casualties?

A Nope. Haven't killed anyone yet.

B Good. That probably puts you in the 99th percentile.

A At least.

B Keep it up, and you can start teaching other people to drive.

A Yeah, uh … let me get my license first.

B Details, details. Why wait till the last minute?

A Yeah, yeah, yeah. So how about you? Did you sign up for Driver's Ed?

B Yeah. I …uh… missed a few sessions. It's pretty good, though.

A What kind of things are you doing?

B To tell you the truth, I like the movies best. Almost as good as my video games.

A But you're getting behind the wheel, right?

B Uh, a little, but I get kinda nervous …

A That's normal.

B I don't like being out on the road with all those crazy drivers.

A That's the only way to get practical experience. We gotta practice as much as we can under real world conditions.

B I'd rather practice it like a video game. It's a lot more fun that way.

A I hope you're still joking.

B No. Totally serious. My video game has better graphics than the windshield.

A Better graphics?

B Much better. The colors are better too. More realistic.

A Reality check. Reality check.

B Reality is for people who can't handle a controller.

A Yeah, uh … I better get going. My mom's calling me. It's … uh, time for our driving lesson.

B She's calling you? I don't hear anything.

A That's because she's back home on Planet Earth.

How Do You Spell Muskrat?

A How do you spell "muskrat?"

B Spell what?

A Muskrat.

B I don't know. What kind of a rat is it?

A It's not a rat. It's like a fox or an owl or something.

B I never heard of such an animal, and I don't know how to spell it.

A Can you look it up for me?

B No! Why don't you look it up?

A Because I don't even know how to spell it.

B Well, I don't know how to spell it, either, and I don't even think it's real.

A It's definitely real, and it's a very important animal.

B You're sure it's not any kind of a rat?

A Yes. I'm not one hundred per cent sure it's a fox or an owl, though. It may be more closely related to the hedge-hog family.

B Are you making all this up?

A No! I'm telling you that you have to help me!

B Why?

A I have to write a paper!

B So why did you pick this stupid topic?!

A It's not stupid! The muskrat is an extremely important and significant animal.

B Says who?

A Says everybody!

B What makes him so important?

A He's right at the top of the food chain!

B Who told you that?

A My teacher!

B How does she know? Does she raise muskrats or something?

A I don't know what she does at home.

B Well, find out!

A I don't care what she does in her free time! I just know I have to write this report, and you have to help me.

B Why me? Why do I get muskrat duty?

A Because you're my friend!

B Some friend. You throw me to the muskrats.

A And everybody else said no.

B Aha!

A Why "Aha?"

B I'm your last choice! Thanks a lot!

A I'm sorry. I should have asked you first.

B   That's okay.

A   It is?!

B   Yeah. I'll help you.

A   You will?!!

B   Come on.

A   Where we going?

B   The library. I'm driving you.

A   Thanks. You're a real friend.

B   And if we don't find any muskrats there, I'll take you to the zoo.

Anything Good on TV?

A Anything good on?

B No. I was watching the game, but I turned it off.

A Me too. They were losing bad.

B Wanna see a movie?

A Yeah. How about a comedy?

B I was looking, but I didn't see anything too funny.

A I saw a *really* funny movie last night. Cracked me up.

B What was it about?

A About two hours.

B No, I mean….oh, come on!

A Gotcha.

B Hope the movie was funnier than that.

A It was great. It was an old movie, in black and white. Did you ever hear of The Marx Brothers?

B Sure. The three guys that hit each other on the head with the sledge hammers?

A No, that's The Three Stooges.

B Oh, that's right.

A These are The Marx Brothers. They were real brothers, too - Groucho, Harpo, and Chico. They had so many great jokes, they talked so fast, and they got into all these crazy situations. I had to keep rewinding to catch all the funny parts. Otherwise, I would have missed stuff.

B They were really that funny?

A Yeah. Harpo was my favorite. He didn't even talk. He just honked this little horn and everybody understood what he was trying to say.

B Is he a lip reader?

A I don't know if he could really talk or not, but he was acting in the movie like he couldn't talk.

B Must be hard to do.

A But then he also played the harp, and it was so beautiful and so serious.

B I never saw anyone play the harp.

A Me neither. Then the other brother, Chico, played the piano, but he played it really funny – like playing normal with one hand and doing tricks with the other hand.

B Wasn't it boring, though, if it was all black and white? I can't watch stuff in black and white. It gives me the creeps.

A No, I'm telling you, it was great. I wish they'd play some old Marx Brothers shows at school.

B If they're so good, how come I never heard of them?

A Probably because they lived a long time ago, like in the 1930s and 1940s. They were really famous then. But I think most of the kids we know just want to see new movies - whatever just came out.

B You mean like Will Farrell and Jack Black? I love those guys.

A Yeah, me too. Don't get me wrong, the new guys are great. But I think they owe a lot to The Marx Brothers.

B They owe a lot?

A Yeah. The guys doing wild comedy stuff nowadays are awesome. But if you watch The Marx Brothers, it's almost like you're seeing the *pre-history* of funny movies or something. It's hard to explain.

B No, you explain it great. You talked me into it. I'm going to look up your friends The Marx Brothers tonight!

A Really?! Even though they're in black and white?

B I'll wear my rose colored glasses....

Double Feature

A So? Did you watch The Marx Brothers? What did you think?

B Yeah. They're great!

A Really?! You watched them?!

B I know what you were talking about now. Those older comedy actors like The Marx Brothers, and the guys with the sledge hammers ... they opened up a door or something. And because of them ... the newer comedians can jump right through.

A That's exactly what I was trying to say.

B Did you ever wonder who opened up that door for The Marx Brothers?

A Wow.... I never even thought about that.

B Probably some other guys in black and white. Maybe silent movies.

A Could be.

B I wonder if it's Charlie Chaplin.

A Who's that?

B This real old time actor. He was in silent movies.

A Never heard of him. Was he good?

B I never saw his stuff. I told you, I don't like black and white.

A So how do you know about him?

B My dad dressed up like him for Halloween. He has a movie poster with Charlie Chaplin on the wall in his office too.

A Oh. He must really like him. What's the name of the movie?

B It's called "Modern Times." I always thought that was funny because it's so old and they call it "Modern Times."

A That is kinda funny.

B Why don't we get the movie and see if it's any good?

A Sure. I'm up for it.

B We can get one with The Marx Brothers too.

A I think they used to call that a double feature.

B Yeah, two movies for the price of one.

A Used to cost ten cents.

B Probably a lot of money back then.

A Probably so. Okay. We'll have a movie history night.

B Yeah. Might be fun for a change.

A Speaking of change … got any money for the movies?

B Uh … I think we can get those movies for free now.

A I guess that's progress.

B Modern Times.

Going to The Movies

A   A bunch of us are going to the movies tomorrow night. Wanna go?

B   What movie?

A   I Still Get a Thrill When I See Jill.

B   Nah. I don't like those idiotic romantic comedies. I like action movies. Shoot 'em up. Blow 'em up. Smash 'em up.

A   Okay. Anything you want to see? Maybe we'll see an action movie instead.

B   Yeah. I want to see the new Stallone movie, where him and Schwarzenegger shoot up all the bad guys from outer space who come here to take over our planet.

A   I'll pass. It sounds boring.

B   How could it be boring if Schwarzenegger and Stallone are toasting aliens for two hours?

A   How about horror?

B   Some of it's okay, as long as it's not too over the top.

A   Any scary movies you want to see?

B   Not right now. All the horror movies out now are kinda cheesy.

A   Documentaries?

B   Get real.

A   Cartoons?

B How old are we?

A I know, I know, but I'm just trying to make suggestions.

B Well, suggest something somebody would actually want to see.

A Great. I suggest we all go to the multiplex. Then we can split up. Everyone can go see whatever movie they want. Anything at all. All alone. All by themselves.

B Which multiplex?

A I don't know. If we can't agree on a movie, I figure at least we can agree on a multiplex.

B The one off the highway has twelve screens, but the one near my house only has ten screens. How do we –

A Pick a multiplex. Any multiplex.

Nice Shoes

A Nice shoes.

B Thanks.

A Where'd you get 'em?

B At the mall. My dad helped me pick them out.

A Wow. Your dad's getting pretty hip.

B He has his moments.

A My dad would never go shopping for shoes with me.

B Did you ever ask him?

A No.

B Why not?

A I don't know. He doesn't really like to go shopping. He's kinda boring sometimes.

B Maybe he needs a cool new pair of shoes.

A Oh, I get it. So...you're thinking like a father-kid get acquainted shopping day at the mall?

B There's probably worse ways to spend an afternoon.

A I guess. Isn't it kind of embarrassing, though? Shopping for shoes with my dad?

B Who's gonna pay for them?

A My dad.

B Well?

A I don't know. It sounds kinda lame.

B   He wasn't always a dad, was he?

A   No, of course not.

B   He used to be our age once upon a time.

A   Yeah, way back in the 80s.

B   What kinda shoes were cool in the 80s?

A   I don't know. Probably something crazy? Something retro?

B   Kinda like now?

A   I guess.

B   Yep. Everything old is new again.

A   Everything old is new again?

B   Something like that. It's an old song my mom and dad did on the karaoke machine.

A   You sing karaoke with your mom and dad?

B   Yeah, but I don't recommend it. Start slowly. Shop for shoes, and work your way up to karaoke.

Is It Cold Outside?

A Is it cold out?

B Kinda cold, but it's not too bad.

A Do you think I need a jacket?

B Nah. You should be okay.

A But you've got a jacket.

B Me? But I'm always cold. Besides, I was just eating ice cream. So I'm extra chilly today.

A Chilly? Maybe I should take a light jacket or a little sweater.

B No, I don't think you need a sweater. You'll be okay.

A But what if it rains?

B It's not going to rain.

A Are you sure?

B Yeah. It's all clear today.

A But it feels humid. It looks cloudy.

B Bring a jacket, a sweater, a hat, gloves, an umbrella, your cell phone, a book, and some cupcakes.

A Why a book and the cell phone? Why are you telling me to bring cupcakes?

B Because I'm not driving you home if you're going to act like this all day. You can call a ride, read your book, and eat your little cupcakes until they come get you.

A Should I bring a pen or a highlighter?

B Why?

A In case I want to write down important passages from my book.

B I changed my mind.

A About what?

B I'm not going out today.

A Why not?

B It's too cold.

A Maybe you should bring a jacket.

Do You Want a Piece of Gum?

A Do you want a piece of gum?

B Sure. Thanks.

A Oh, wait! Wow. I'm sorry…

B Sorry about what?

A I can't give you a piece of gum after all.

B Why not?

A I only have one piece left.

B Okay.

A Okay what?

B Okay, so give me that one piece. One piece is all I need. I'm not one of those people that chews more than one piece of gum. My little brother chews two or three at a time, but I think that's just too much.

A I can't.

B Why not?

A Because I was going to chew this piece of gum myself.

B What do you mean?

A I was planning to have it after lunch. I specifically had this stick of gum scheduled for math class.

B But … you specifically asked me if I wanted a piece of gum.

A Yeah. I didn't think you were going to say yes. So what?

B So why did you do that?

A I was just trying to be nice.

B Well, it's not working. You're not being nice.

A Well, that's kinda rude. How am I not nice?

B Because now I want a piece of stupid gum, and you're telling me I can't have one!

A What? Am I the only source for chewing gum around here?

B I sure hope not.

A What's that supposed to mean?

B It means I want a piece of gum.

A And I can't give you what I don't have. Your chewing gum needs are not my responsibility. Is there a sign around my neck that says "Wrigley's?"

B Nope.

A Good. There are plenty of other places a resourceful person can find gum.

B Look, just relax, okay? I don't want to argue with you.

A Good.

B Tell you what. Let's just tear that piece of gum in half, okay? We'll share.

A I don't think so!

B You won't even give me half a stick of gum?

A There's a vending machine down the hall. Use it!

Are You Dating?

A Are you dating anyone?

B No, not really. Not right now.

A Why not?

B I don't know. I want to stay focused. I've got school, basketball practice, study group.

A So what?

B Lots of other good stuff to concentrate on.

A Yeah, but you can still be seeing someone.

B Plenty of time for that later. I don't want to get distracted.

A What is it they say about all work and no play?

B I don't know. I was working when they were playing.

A Very funny. Ha. Ha. Ha.

B But I'm serious. Remember when my older brother broke up with his girlfriend? Right before finals last year?

A Yeah, I remember. He was with Stephanie, right?

B Right. He got so depressed he totally bombed out on his final exams.

A Really?

B Yeah. He was so sad and down and gloomy. I don't want that to be me. I don't need all that stress.

A Yeah, but you still have to socialize.

B That's not why we're here. That's not why I'm going to school.

A Man, oh man. You're not kidding when you talk about focus.

B There's three kinds of people in the world. People who make things happen, people who watch what happens, and people who wonder what happened.

A Hey, that's good.

B Guess which group I want to be in.

A I'm guessing the first one.

B I'm guessing you're right.

Sam's Party

A Hey.

B Hey. Hey.

A Are you going to the party Saturday?

B Uh, I don't know … will Alex be there?

A Sure.

B Oh, great …

A Why do you say it like that? Alex is so nice. I love Alex.

B Because Alex is always hanging all over Sam! Acting all chummy – chummy …

A Of course! They're cousins!

B What?! How do you know that?

A I don't remember. I think I drove Alex to Sam's house one time. Alex kept calling Sam's father Uncle Dan.

B You're kidding me!

A No. Alex's mother and Sam's father are sister and brother. I think that's how they're related.

B Oh! I thought they were together. I thought they were boyfriend and girlfriend or something!

A No way! What made you even think that?

B I don't know. He's always driving her home, and they're always hanging out together.

A Yeah….kinda like….uh….cousins.

B Wow, now I'm really embarrassed…

A Nah. Don't be embarrassed. Jumping to conclusions is great exercise!

B Don't tell anybody, okay?

A No worries.

B So ... yes.

A Yes what?

B Yes, I'm going to the party Saturday.

Can You Cook a Chicken?

A Do you know how to cook a chicken?

B Is it dead already?

A Of course it's dead! What do you think?

B I don't know!

A You think I went to the store and bought a *live* chicken?

B How should I know what you bought? Why are you asking me all these questions, anyway?

A I want to cook a chicken!

B So go ahead and cook it.

A I don't know how! You have to help me!

B Since when are you so interested in cooking chickens?

A My mom and dad are coming home late tonight, and I want to surprise them with something. I thought it would be nice to cook for them.

B That *is* nice.

A Thank you.

B You're welcome. But I can't help you cook a chicken.

A Do you know how to cook anything else? I want to make them something good and tasty. A nice surprise.

B I know how to make some stuff to eat, but I don't know how to cook any of it.

A What can you make?

B   I can make all kinds of good sandwiches, like tuna salad, chicken salad, and peanut butter and jelly.

A   How about egg salad?

B   How *about* egg salad?

A   Do you know how to *make* egg salad?

B   No, but it can't be that hard. We should be able to figure it out together.

A   Okay. My parents like egg salad. I think they do. I hope they do.

B   So we probably need eggs, mayo, and maybe bread.

A   Definitely bread. How about veggies? Should we chop up some veggies for inside the egg salad?

B   Yeah, I think you're supposed to have celery in it.

A   No, that's tuna salad.

B   Oh, that's right.

A   So what kind of vegetable goes in egg salad?

B   Maybe carrots.

A   Yeah, it must be carrots.

B   Sounds like a pain, chopping up carrots. Don't your parents like pizza?

A   Sure. Everybody likes pizza.

B   Why don't you just order a pizza?

A Okay. That's a pretty good surprise too, right?

B Right.

A Can you *help* me order the pizza?

B Okay. Do you need money?

A No. I think I have enough. How much does a pizza cost?

B I think about ten, twelve bucks.

A Okay. Can I borrow a few dollars?

B How much?

A Ten. Maybe eleven, eleven-fifty. Better make it twelve. Yeah, twelve should do it.

Choir Practice

A   Hey, where are you going?

B   Choir practice. Wanna come?

A   No. I can't carry a tune in a bucket!

B   Don't put yourself down.

A   I'm just being realistic.

B   Reality is for people with no imagination.

A   Listen, when we sing *Happy Birthday* around the dinner table, the rest of my family asks me to mouth the words.

B   Doesn't matter. It's a skill you can develop. Michael Jordan got cut from his high school basketball team.

A   He got cut for being a bad singer?

B   No! For being a bad basketball player! He practiced and became better.

A   You know, talking to you is like trying to nail scrambled eggs to a tree. It doesn't stick.

B   Can't help it. I see you in the choir. I can see it!

A   Will you please drop it?

B   I just know you'll be great. I can *see you* being great.

A   Stop it already!

B   As a matter of fact, I see you as the lead soloist in the choir.

A   I see you in my rear view mirror.

B   Hey, what's that supposed to mean?

A   It means *hasta la vista, baby!*

Drama Club

A   Hey, are you going to try out for the school play?

B   No, what's that?

A   The school play! The drama club puts it on. They have posters up everywhere. You didn't hear about the school play?

B   I think this is the first time I've heard about it.

A   It's going to be great. You've got to come audition with me.

B   Nah. I don't want to do that. It sounds stupid.

A   But how do you know if you don't try?

B   My older brother was in a school play once. It was some boring Shakespeare play. We all went to see him, and he was just standing around in the background holding a spear.

A   Maybe he had fun.

B   How could he have fun carrying a spear?

A   I don't know. It's what you make of it. I think anything can be fun if you have the right mindset.

B   The right mindset?

A   Sure. Besides, it's acting. You have to use your imagination sometimes.

B   It's depressing, though, isn't it?

A   Why would it be depressing?

B My mother says there's a broken heart for every light on Broadway.

A I'm not talking about Broadway. I'm just going in to audition for our own school play. Right here in the auditorium.

B But ... aren't people who do acting kind of weird?

A What do you mean?

B Don't they do all kind of crazy exercises in acting class ... like telling you to pretend to be a tree ... or act like a piece of bacon sizzling in the frying pan?

A I don't know. I never heard about any of that stuff.

B I think that's how they rehearse.

A Look, I just thought it would be fun to be on stage in a school play.

B My brother said they made him be a Snickers bar once.

A Well ... I don't know about that. But ... I guess if you have to be a candy bar, you may as well be a Snickers.

Democrats and Republicans

A I can't wait till I'm old enough to vote.

B Not me.

A Why not?

B My father never votes. He thinks it's stupid.

A What's stupid about it?

B I don't know. He says the Democrats and the Republicans are all the same, and it doesn't matter who you vote for because they all do bad things anyway.

A My dad always votes. He says it's our civic duty.

B What does that mean?

A I think it means we have to do good things and take care of stuff because we're citizens of the United States or something.

B But what happens if you vote, and the guy you vote for doesn't win?

A That happens sometimes because we can't win at everything we try.

B Just like sports.

A That's right. But we still have to keep trying.

B But what if you vote for somebody and he wins, but he ends up being no good? You know what I mean?

A Yeah. My father says there's always a chance that can happen, because some people aren't so good at their jobs.

B Like that guy from the pizza place.

A I know! The guy with the big, smelly beard! He's so rude! He's rude to all the customers.

B He's definitely not good at his job.

A I hate going to that place.

B Me too. They have pretty good pizza, but I don't like going there because of him.

A I would never vote for that guy.

B Me neither.

A But I would vote for some other guys with beards … like Abraham Lincoln if he was still alive.

B Yeah, me too. Abraham Lincoln had a beard, but not a big, smelly one.

A Abraham Lincoln had a nice beard.

B I'd vote for Lincoln if I was old enough. I bet my father would even vote for him.

A And if President Lincoln worked in a pizza place, he'd be nice to everybody.

B That's why he's on the penny.

Trimming Down

A Wanna get some lunch?

B No, not today.

A Did you eat already?

B No, I'm fasting today.

A Fasting?

B Yeah, I'd like to drop a few pounds.

A So ... you're not eating anything?

B Right. I'm drinking water, but I'm not eating anything.

A Not even a salad?

B Not even a cracker.

A I don't know about this. I don't think this is such a good idea.

B It's a great idea.

A Sounds like you're messing around with your health. That's dangerous.

B It's dangerous to be carrying around extra weight. *That's* dangerous.

A Well, I think you look fine.

B I don't look fine.

A You do. Who's putting all this junk in your head?

B Look, I need to drop a few. That's it.

A But I'm telling you - you look great just like you are.

B Do I look as good as the kids on the swim team? How about Sam? Do I look as good as Sam? The truth.

A Come on! We can all look better, but –

B See! You admit it!

A Okay, okay, okay! Nobody looks as good as Sam! So what?

B So it means I have to trim down. So that's what I'm doing.

A But we don't have to try crazy diets and fasting!

B Yes, we do!

A No, we don't! Everyone's body is different.

B Cut the calories, and we lose the weight. That's the same with everybody! No food, no calories, no extra weight, no body fat! No problem!

A No kidding.

B No food. No nothin'.

A No clue.

Macaroni and Peas

A Hey, what's for dinner tonight?

B I think we're having macaroni and peas.

A I think you mean macaroni and cheese.

B No. Peas. Mom wants us to eat more vegetables.

A Eeeewww!!! That's disgusting!!

B No, it's not. It sounds good to me.

A What's good about it?

B Well, peas are green. You've got macaroni that's light colored, maybe a pale yellow or an off-white. That's a very nice color combination.

A Who cares about the color? It's what the food tastes like that's important!

B Says who?!

A Says me!

B But it has to look nice.

A Only if we're going to be on one of those crazy cooking shows on TV.

B Oh, I wish!

A Why?

B: All the food they make looks so pretty! It looks so nice! It's so attractive!

A You know what?

B What?

A: I don't care what my food looks like!

B Well, you should. The presentation of a meal is very important.

A My food can be ugly. I'll settle for a big, fat, ugly cheeseburger.

B Oooh, that sounds delicious!

A: Yeah!

B What color?

A What?

B What color cheese? White or yellow?

A I don't know! Cheese color cheese!

B What color burger and bun?

A Cheeseburger color!

B What color plate will you serve it on?

A Mom!!

Wanna Grab a Bite?

A   Hungry?

B   Always.

A   Let's grab a cheeseburger.

B   No. I don't eat red meat anymore. Remember?

A   Oh, yeah. I forgot. But you can get a veggie burger, maybe a turkey burger.

B   Yeah, but I'm trying to avoid all that bread. Really trying to cut back on carbs.

A   Wanna just get a soda, then?

B   No! Are you kidding me? No carbonated drinks.

A   Okay.

B   Ever!

A   Okay!

B   And you know how much sugar is in a twenty-ounce bottle of soda?

A   I think I'm gonna find out…

B   One bottle has sixteen grams of sugar. That's sixteen of those little individual sugar packets. That's crazy, right?

A   Definitely crazy. Can we do a diet soda?

B   Artificial sweetener. You know how many laboratory rats they've killed with those artificial sweeteners? It's been proven. They've known this for 30 years. They don't care.

A Coffee? Latte? Mocha? Espresso? Cappuccino? Mochachino?

B Can't. Caffeine gives me the jitters. You know that. I'll be up all night.

A Okay, I got it. How about a nice big salad from the cafeteria?

B Pesticides. You like eating bug spray? If you eat one of those salads from the cafeteria, you may as well use bug spray for your salad dressing.

A Uh … I guess I'll pass on the salad …

B Yeah, I don't blame you.

A How about some nice, cold bottled water?

B I don't like it too cold. Hurts my throat.

A Room temperature, then?

B That sounds great.

A Terrific. Glad we can agree on something.

B I know! You're always such a picky eater!

Please Rate
Your Customer Service

A Why am I getting all these weird phone calls?

B Like what?

A Like today. I bought something at this new store yesterday, and today I get a call from some company asking me to rate their customer service.

B So what?

A So it's annoying, that's what.

B I think it's nice.

A It's not nice.

B They probably just want to make sure you're satisfied with the whole experience.

A I *was* satisfied until they started annoying me with all their stupid questions.

B They're just trying to see if you're happy with their service.

A If I bought something and didn't return it, then that means I'm happy with their service. Period. End of story.

B I think you need to lighten up.

A No, they need to *tighten* up. They need to get their act together and stop bothering their customers.

B Why don't you tell them to put you on their Do Not Call list?

A   Because then they'll call and ask me to rate the service I receive from the representative who puts my name on the Do Not Call list.

B   Maybe you should just shop online from now on.

A   Then they'll call and ask me to rate the service of my Internet provider.

B   Maybe you should stop shopping entirely, then.

A   Well ... no ... I don't want to do that.

B   Can I help you with anything else today?

A   What? No, uh ... I don't think so.

B   Have I exceeded your expectations today?

A   Uh ... what? What are you ...

B   Press "one" for yes. Press "two" for no ...

A   Arrrghhh!!!

Tattoo and a Nose Ring

A I'm thinking more and more about getting a tattoo.

B Uh....I don't think you should do that.

A Why not? I need to change my style. Kick it up a notch.

B Nah. Tattoos are permanent. You might not like it in a few years. Even a few months.

A Maybe you're right.

B Trust me. Try something simple, like a new haircut or a pair of cool shoes.

A Maybe a nose ring...

B I don't think so.

A Lip ring?

B Looks painful.

A Belly button ring?

B I'm not a fan. I just don't think that's very sanitary.

A You're not being very encouraging, you know.

B This might be one of those things you'll thank me for later.

A I don't see it.

B You will.

A How about a toe ring?

B A toe ring is okay.

A Will you help me pick one out?

B Sure. I know if the toe ring were on the other foot, you'd help me too.

A Thanks.

B They've got some nice ones at that little jewelry store in the mall.

A Okay. Let's go.

B Cool.

A I think we'll pass a tattoo place on the way to the mall.

B No, we won't. We're taking the long way.

No More Texting!

A Guess what?

B What?

A I've got big news!

B Tell me!!

A It's my New Year's resolution. I'm giving up texting!

B Yeah, right.

A I'm serious.

B Did your phone break?

A Nope. My phone is perfect.

B Did your parents change their cell plan?

A Not that I know of.

B You feeling okay?

A Never better. I just realized I'm texting too much.

B So what?

A I don't want to be like everyone else. Texting all the time, all distracted, never paying attention to what's going on. I'm sick of it. We all text too much. My Aunt Mollie says people don't even know how to talk to each other anymore. I think she's right.

B What'd you say? I wasn't really paying attention.

A Come on. I'm being serious. I'm trying to talk to you about something important.

B   Sorry.

A   It's okay. Nobody takes me seriously about this ...

B   No. I'm listening to what you're saying.

A   Really?

B   Yeah. It may not be what I want to hear, but it may be exactly what I need to hear.

A   Hey, thanks. I appreciate it.

B   No prob. As a matter of fact, I'm going to join you in this worthy cause.

A   Really?

B   Yep. I promise. I'm not gonna text any more.

A   Wonderful. That's great!

B   I'm not gonna text any less, but I'm not gonna text any more!

Never Complain,
Never Explain

A   You feeling any better today?

B   Not really. Still sniffling... achy... got headaches.... runny nose.

A   You know what they say, "if your nose runs and your feet smell, you may be built upside down."

B   Cut it out. You're not even funny.

A   C'mon. I'm just trying to cheer you up.

B   Well, you're not.

A   Snap out of it. Don't go around feeling sorry for yourself. It's not good.

B   Leave me alone! I don't feel well!

A   Complaining about it won't make you feel any better.

B   I'm not complaining!

A   Never complain. Never explain.

B   Why are you picking on me when I don't feel good? You hear the other kids at school go on and on and on about all of their stuff? And how about our math teacher? She's always griping and moaning about every stupid, goofball thing that happens to her. But do you say anything about them? No! But I tell you I have a headache and you jump all over me. They're okay, but I'm not okay?

A   Now it sounds like you're complaining about how much other people complain.

B Okay, I give up. Please just stop talking to me, and I'll probably start feeling better. As a matter of fact, yeah, I feel better already. Okay? Happy? It's all good. I feel better now.

A Good, better, best. Never let it rest. Until your good is better, and your better is best.

B Okay … if you stop with the stupid jokes and sayings, I'll stop complaining.

A Great. I'm just trying to help. Trying to take your mind off your troubles.

B I know.

A Good. I'm not picking on you. I'm not trying to be annoying. I just want to get you back to your old, friendly, normal self.

B I know. I appreciate your trying to help.

A Good. That's what friends are for. You follow me?

B Yeah.

A Don't follow me. I'll call the cops.

Summer Job

A What are you doing this summer?

B Nothing much. How about you?

A Got my first job.

B Really?!

A Yeah. I want to start making my own money.

B Awesome! What kind of work are you doing?

A Got a job at the football stadium.

B No kidding! I love football!

A Me too!

B Me three! Can you get me a job there?

A I'll bring you an application tomorrow.

B What kind of work are you doing at the stadium?

A It's a great job! I put the cheese in all the mousetraps!

B Gross!

A Baby! What the matter? Afraid of mice?

B No, I'm lactose intolerant.

A Oh. Sorry.

B Thanks. But it's still gross.

A Thanks a lot! It's a very important job, you know!

B Forget my application!

A Good!

B Good!

A Fine!

B Fine! I don't like football anyway!

A   Yes you do!

B Not anymore!

Babysitting

A Wanna hit the coffee shop?

B Can't. Babysitting in a little while.

A What are you doing that for?

B Just making a little extra money. You know.

A But your parents are both lawyers, right?

B Yeah, so what?

A They must be making good money.

B I guess they are. So?

A So why do you have to go to work?

B I don't have to. I want to. I like to make my own money. It's kinda fun.

A Why?

B I don't like to ask mom and dad for money every time I want to buy something.

A But they're both lawyers! They must be so rich.

B Not all lawyers are rich.

A But you live in such a nice house.

B Thanks. But what does that have to do with my babysitting?

A Everything. The dinky little money you're gonna make tonight is probably like one drip of water compared to what your parents make.

B It's not so dinky. It's pretty good pocket money.

A Compared to what your parents make?

B: It doesn't matter how much they make or don't make. I like my babysitting jobs, and I think it's good practice for being out in the real world.

A You don't need this. Plenty of time to work when we're older.

B I'll work when I'm older. I'll work when I'm younger. What's the big deal?

A I think you're putting way too much pressure on yourself.

B Why all this interest in my babysitting job tonight?

A Because I want to go to the coffee shop!

B So go to the coffee shop! Who's stopping you?

A You are! You have your stupid little job. So now I have to go get coffee alone.

B You know what?

A No, I don't!

B Sounds like you need a babysitter.

How Many Presidents?

A What are you reading?

B A story about George Washington.

A Really? Do you know how many Presidents there have been?

B I don't know. I remember when President Obama was elected. I think he was number forty-four.

A Right. Because President Bush was number forty-three.

B How many can you name off the top of your head?

A Good question. Probably ten or twelve, I think.

B Okay, that's not bad. Who are they?

A Well … we already said Washington, Bush, and Obama.

B That's three. Who else?

A I saw that movie about Abraham Lincoln.

B Okay, but that's still only four.

A There's the other two guys on Mount Rushmore. Thomas Jefferson and the guy with the glasses.

B What guy with the glasses?

A Oh, man, what was his name again? Oh, uh … Theodore Roosevelt!

B Oh, yeah! Speak softly but carry a big stick.

A Right, and there's Bush's father too!

B Yeah, I forgot about him! What number was he?

A He was forty-one.

B But how can you even remember that?

A I always remember because Bush used to call his father "forty-one." That was a nickname for his dad. And he called his mother "one."

B That's pretty funny! But … then who was number forty-two?

A Come on! Bill Clinton!

B Right, right, right! How could I forget him?!

A I don't know! How could you?

B How could anyone?!

Christmas Presents

A What are you getting for Christmas?

B I don't know. It's supposed to be a surprise.

A Yeah, but you can find out, can't you?

B Probably, but that would ruin the surprise.

A Aren't you curious?

B Nope.

A Why not?

B I know where my mom and dad hide the presents. It's always the same place – the hall closet - but I don't want to spoil the surprise.

A Wow. I wouldn't be able to sleep if I knew where the presents were hidden in *my* house. You know what I mean?

B Yep.

A Doesn't it bother you?

B Nope.

A Not even a little?

B Nope.

A Are you sure?

B Yep.

A Positive?

B Yep.

A Not a teeny bit curious?

B Nope.

A Really?

B Yep.

A Will you show me where they are?

B Nope.

A Not a big talker today, huh?

B Nope.

A You're not mad at me, though, are you?

B Mad? Why?

A For asking all these questions.

B No. Nope.

A Are you getting tired of my questions, though?

B A little, but it's okay.

A You sure?

B Yep.

A Looking forward to Christmas?

B Yep.

A And you're really not going to show me those presents?

B Nope.

You Should Get The New One

A Is that your phone?

B Yeah. Why?

A It's so old.

B It's okay. It's my mom's old one. I like it.

A Your mom got the new one?

B Yeah. She gave me her old one. My dad got the new one too, and he gave his old one to my little sister.

A That's not right. You should all get the new one. The whole family should get the new one.

B Why?

A Duh! Because it's new.

B So what?

A It's got all the new features and updates.

B This one's fine. I really like it.

A Really? You *really* like it?

B Yeah. I always liked it when my mom had it. But I like it even better now.

A Why?

B Because I have it.

A But it's old.

B It works great.

A It's practically an antique.

B If you say so.

A Hey, uh … is that a little crack in the corner of the screen?

B A little one, but you can hardly see it. It still works fine.

A Aren't you embarrassed to use that phone?

B Nope.

A All your friends have the new one.

B That's nice.

A Your friends will think you're poor. They might be embarrassed for you.

B Then they're not my friends.

A Listen, I'm just going to be straight with you, because you're obviously not getting it, and you need someone to step in and do an intervention.

B Don't you think you're overreacting a little?

A Not when you show up with an old phone like that. You have to get rid of it immediately - if not sooner.

B Why?

A Because it's old.

B But I like it.

A Maybe you can donate it to a museum.

B I like it.

A If they'll even take it. You probably have to drop it off at the back door. Maybe after hours.

A Part-Time Dog

A What's the matter?

B Nothing.

A You look sad. Are you upset about something?

B I don't know. I want to get a dog, but my mom says we can't have one.

A Why don't you ask your dad?

B Because he always says to ask my mom.

A That's the same thing *my* dad always says!

B Yeah, and then he always does whatever my mom says anyway.

A Not my dad. He doesn't do anything my mom says.

B You're lucky.

A But maybe your mom has a good reason. Does she say why? Is she afraid of dogs?

B No, she's not afraid. She says dogs are a lot of work, and they're messy, and they're expensive and everything.

A Well, that's kinda true. She's kinda right about that.

B Yeah, but I still want one. They're so friendly.

A I know.

B They're so funny. I love dogs.

A Me too.

B So how do I get one?

A Well… maybe if you can't have one of your own, you can get a part-time dog!

B A part-time dog?

A Sure.

B What is he when he's not a dog – a cat?

A No! He's always a dog! You just don't have him all the time! Only part- time!

B How do I get a part-time dog?

A You volunteer. You go down to the shelter or the vet or the groomer and ask them if you can help out with the dogs.

B You think I could do that? You think they'd let me?

A Sure. You can even get a part-time job at a pet shop.

B A part-time pet shop?

A No, a full-time pet shop. They'll pay you to help with the dogs. That's what my Aunt Tammy does. My Aunt Adele just started too. They love dogs, but they don't want to clean up after one at home.

B Okay, I guess I could try to do the same thing.

A Why not? You like dogs, and that's where they keep them. So go where the dogs are.

B Good point.

A Besides, there's plenty of good dogs out there that need your help.

B   I know!

A   Get yourself a part-time dog. You can even have a whole
    bunch of different dogs if they're all part-time.

B   I'm glad you're not a part-time friend.

A   Ruff ! Ruff !!

B   Grrrrrrr !!!

Drama Scenes

Adopted

A   Are you sure?

B   Positive.

A   How'd you find out?

B   They told me.

A   How? When?

B   Yesterday. Showed me all kinds of old papers.

A   That's so weird to me. I mean, you look so much like your mom. Exactly.

B   Except she's not my mom anymore.

A   What are you going to do?

B   I don't know. I have to do something. Maybe I don't have to do something. I don't even know at this point. I don't know what to do. I really don't.

A   In a way, you know, you're … really lucky … really fortunate.

B   I'm lucky? How am I lucky? Dumped by my real parents before I could walk or talk. Dropped off at some stupid government office. Dumped. Dumped like a bag of garbage. Does that sound lucky? Real lucky. I'm a walking, talking, four-leaf clover.

A   You know, I hate to tell you … but I think you're missing something here.

B   What am I missing — except my real mother and my real father?

A   You're looking at what you don't have. You're missing what you do have.

B   What do I have?

A   Figure it out. Don't think about the parents who gave you up. Think about the ones who raised you. You've got a mom and dad who *picked* you. That means they *selected* you.

B   So?

A   Most everybody else got the parents they have ... not by choice. It's just how they were born. But out of all the kids in the world, the parents you grew up with, who raised you ... picked *you.*

B   But I don't even know who I am now. I don't know what my real name is.

A   Well, what's in a name, really? People change their names all the time. Even sports teams change their names. A name's not such a big deal.

B   You're just not going to let me off the hook, are you?

A   What do you mean?

B   How can you always be so up? I can't do it. I keep thinking of all the reasons I have to be depressed about this, but you're so positive.

A   We have to be positive – as much as we can, anyway.

B   I'm trying, I'm trying.

A   I don't care what your name is. Your name doesn't change who you are. Neither do your parents.

B I know.

A I'll make a deal with you. You can change your name every day if you want, and I'll still be your best friend.

B Do you think I should look for my natural parents?

A I don't know. What do your folks say?

B They said they'll help me if I want to find them.

A Sounds like they really love you. Sounds like they support you no matter what.

B Yeah, they do. I think they definitely do.

A Sounds like pretty good parents to me.

B Yeah. Me too.

Helping The Homeless

A My class is going on a field trip this weekend. They said we can bring someone. Wanna go?

B Yeah. Cool. Where you going?

A A homeless shelter. We're all going to volunteer.

B That kinda stinks. Why?

A My teacher does a lot of work with homeless organizations. She volunteers at a soup kitchen every Thanksgiving and every Christmas. That's why she invited us to bring a friend. The more the better.

B Not me. No thanks.

A Why? Are you busy?

B Not really. I just don't want to go to a place like that.

A Why not?

B I hate homeless people. They smell so nasty. They're always bothering everybody, asking for money. Standing in the middle of the road holding those stupid cardboard signs.

A I can't even believe what's coming out of your mouth. That is so disrespectful.

B Why should I respect them? They're a bunch of losers.

A No, they're a bunch of people. They're human beings.

B Don't look like it. Sure don't smell like it.

A Put yourself in their shoes. You might feel differently.

B No thanks.

A Everybody needs help sometimes. Some people just need a little more.

B Yeah, junkies and alcoholics.

A Maybe some. But lots of them are regular people who just got into bad situations.

B Yeah, by drinking and shooting up.

A That's really rude.

B It's the truth.

A No. Some are battered women who had to run away from their husbands. Some are people who lost their jobs, or got sick, and then got kicked out of their houses and apartments.

B That's their stupid fault.

A There are even homeless kids.

B Kids?

A Yeah, kids just like us. Except they have parents who can't take care of them.

B Can't or won't?

A Maybe half and half. Can't say it's the kids' stupid fault though, can you?

B No, I guess not.

A These kids didn't do anything wrong, didn't hurt anybody. They still ended up homeless, in a bad situation that they didn't create.

B   So ... uh, what do they do?

A   I don't know. I guess they just do their best, like we do.

B   What do you mean?

A   They go to school, and try not to let their problems mess them up too much. Everybody has problems, right? Some just need a little more help to fix them.

B   But how can they study and do their homework in a homeless shelter?

A   I really don't know. It must be hard.

B   What do they feed kids in a place like that?

A   I don't know. Why don't you come with me and we'll find out?

B   This weekend?

A   Yeah. Saturday. We'll be there all day, but you can just come for an hour or two if you want. That would be a big help.

B   That's okay. I'll go with you.

A   You will? That's great.

B   And ... uh, I don't have to leave after just an hour. I can stay there all day with you guys.

College Night

A Are you going to the college night thing?

B Yeah, I guess. It's so confusing.

A I know.

B How do you decide which college? There's so many. They're so far away. They're so expensive.

A I was even thinking maybe I'll just go to a community college first so I don't have to pick a four-year school.

B Yeah, but then you still have to decide the same thing in two years anyway, so you may as well pick one now.

A I guess so, but I can't even decide what my major is going to be.

B Me neither. It might not matter for the first two years, though. We can probably take all the intro classes and that should help us decide.

A But we can take intro classes at the community college, and we can stay home.

B Don't you want to go away to school?

A I think so, but it's a little scary too.

B You've been away from home before. Summer camp. Sports camp.

A This is different, though. It's all new people to meet.

B I know.

A It just feels like everything's so much … bigger.

B Bigger and harder.

A There are schools with something like thirty thousand enrolled.

B That's crazy, right?

A It's like you're just a number.

B My older sister says everybody feels like that. If there's thirty thousand, all of them must feel like numbers too.

A So that means we have something in common?

B I guess so.

A Maybe it's normal.

B Everything new is kinda scary anyway.

A So if we're doing something scary, we'll have company, right?

B With all those people going to college —

A We've gotta find some cool people to hang out with.

B Maybe even your roommate. They can't all be jerks.

A But how do you know that?

B We're gonna be there and we're not jerks.

A That makes sense.

B So maybe they're just like us.

Go For a Run?

A   Wanna run tonight?

B   Sure. How far?

A   Down to the duck pond and back. My normal route.

B   You go that far? Sounds kinda far.

A   About four miles.

B   I don't think I'll make it that far. Can we do a shorter run?

A   How about a couple of times around the reservoir?

B   Yeah, that sounds more my speed.

A   Okay. I might go a couple of extra laps if it's all right with you.

B   Wow. Where'd you get all this energy? You never used to run that far.

A   I've been taking it up a notch since the summer. I get up a half hour early to stretch and do some calisthenics before school too.

B   Doesn't that make you tired?

A   Not really. At first it did, but now it gives me a little more energy.

B   Maybe I should try that. I always get a little tired right after lunch.

A   It might be what you're eating too. I cut out sodas and desserts a couple of months ago, and I feel a thousand times better. A million times better.

B You really feel a difference?

A Definitely. I'm drinking more water too. Water instead of soda.

B Wow. It sounds like any one of those things would work, but if you're doing all of them together....

A Exactly. "All of the above."

B That's amazing.

A I figure if I do "all of the above," I'll look better, feel better, and be a better athlete. I think it's making me a better student too, 'cause I can concentrate better now.

B I changed my mind.

A About what?

B We're running down to the duck pond and back.

A Really? Great!

B I'll bring us a couple of water bottles too.

A Good for you!

B All of the above!

Did You Have a Nice Weekend?

A How was your weekend?

B Stunk.

A Oh, no! Really?

B Yeah, really. Stunk, stunk, stunk, like a drunk old skunk.

A Why? What happened?

B Nothing. That's what stunk it all up.

A So tell me what happened.

B I'm telling you. Nothing happened all weekend. I had nothing going on. Nothing to do, nothing at all.

A Not even homework?

B Not even homework.

A So what did you end up doing?

B I just told you. I had nothing to do all weekend! Nothing. Nada. Zilch. Zip. Zippo.

A Did you go anywhere?

B I didn't go anywhere. I stayed in my room all weekend. It was really depressing too.

A Why didn't you call me? Or call *somebody* to do *something*?

B I figured everyone was busy.

A Why?

B I didn't hear from anybody.

A Well, you don't have to wait to hear from people. You can pick up the phone and call someone yourself.

B Yeah, but they can call me too. If they don't call first, then it's like they're disrespecting me. So why should I call them? Why should I even give them the satisfaction?

A Don't you think you're being a little immature?

B *I'm* immature?

A A little. It's up to us to make our own good time. If we're having a bad day – or even a boring day – it's up to us to work our way out of it. Otherwise, we can get really down and depressed.

B You're wrong. Friends are supposed to be there to help you. If you're feeling down, friends are supposed to call you and invite you to get out and do something fun and cool, so you aren't locked up in your room all weekend like Rapunzel.

A Sorry to break this to you, Rapunzel, but you need to let your hair down and invite the world in once in a while.

B You know... I don't appreciate your attitude today.

A Look, we all live on a two-way street. Traffic goes both ways.

B I'm *glad* you didn't call me this weekend.

A Wow. Just wow.

B Yeah. Wow.

Cheerleading Tryouts

A Are you ready to try out for the cheer squad Friday?

B I don't know.

A You don't know? You were so excited last week.

B I'm not so sure anymore.

A It's an easy question. A or B. Yes or no.

B It's not so easy. I'm not sure I want to be a cheerleader now.

A Why not?

B Just stuff people say…

A What do people say?

B Everybody says cheerleaders are stupid. They're not serious. They're all party girls… party boys … party, party, party …

A Who's everybody? Who's telling you all this stuff? I didn't hear any of this.

B Just like everyone.

A Who?!

B Those girls from science class.

A You mean April and Jennifer and all them?

B Yeah. But not just them.

A Who else?

B Kids from my neighborhood, neighbors.

A You mean those neighbors who just moved in?

B Yeah.

A Why do you care what they think? You don't even know them, do you?

B No, not really all that well, I guess.

A You guess or you know?

B I guess I know...

A I know you know! And don't even get me started on Jennifer and April. They are so *rude*. They've got to be two of the rudest, most disrespectful kids in the whole school. Them and their whole clique.

B Maybe you're right...

A *Maybe* I'm right? Why do you even care what these people think?

B It's important what people think about you!

A It's not important! It's only important if those people are important to you. Like your family and your close friends. You shouldn't even worry about other people.

B Easy for you to say.

A Easy for you to say too. If you live your life to please other people then you're not being real. You're not the person you're supposed to be. You have to be the real you.

B What do you mean "the real you?"

A There's only one of you in the whole world, and you have to be the real one. No one else can do it for you.

B Wow. How'd you get to be so smart?

A   By trying to figure out how to be the real me.

B   Well ... I think the real you is pretty cool.

A   Aw ... you're just saying that because it's true!

B   It is true!

Splitting Up

A Why do you keep yawning? You keep yawning, stretching.

B Up late.

A Why?

B Couldn't sleep.

A Are you worried about something? You seem a little distracted lately.

B No, not really. Maybe a little worried about my mom and dad, but nothing too bad.

A What's up with your mom and dad? They both okay?

B They're okay, I guess. They just fight a lot.

A I didn't know that. They both seem so nice.

B Yeah, I know. They are nice.

A They're always super-nice to me whenever I come over.

B They're nice to everybody. I just wish they were nicer to each other.

A Really?

B Yeah, they've been fighting all the time.

A All the time?

B Pretty much.

A Not …uh… violent, though, right?

B Oh no, no, no. Nobody hit anybody. Nothing like that.

A What do they fight about?

B Mostly money at first. Then my dad started complaining about my mom's family. Now my mom's arguing with dad's side of the family too.

A Sounds like a lot of stuff going on at your house.

B It's a lot. It's definitely a lot.

A Maybe they need to get some help.

B They might be a little bit beyond help.

A Maybe they can talk to somebody … like a marriage counselor or a clergyman? Somebody should be able to help.

B Well, I think they're just about past all that at this point. I think they've run through most of their options.

A What does that mean?

B My dad's moving out. He got an apartment.

A Oh …. no … I'm sorry …

B My mom and dad's marriage is pretty much over, I think.

A Any chance they … uh … might work it out?

B I wish. I'm pretty sure it's over.

A I'm really sorry. I don't even know what to say.

B There's not much to say.

A You know it has nothing to do with you, right? I mean, it's not your fault or anything. You know that, right? A lot of kids feel guilty.

B Oh, I know. This has been coming for a long time. They just don't love each other any more.

A Wow. What about you and your brothers?

B I think for now we're staying with my mom.

A Well.. if you need anything …

B I'm okay … but I'll let you know … thanks …

A What are you doing now?

B Nothing. Nothing much right now.

A Wanna get something to eat?

B No, that's okay. I'm not too hungry.

A C'mon, you've gotta eat. At least have a soda with me.

B Well. Sure, we can do that. That sounds good. Thanks.

A You'll get through this.

B Thanks.

The English Paper

A How's your English paper coming along?

B It's not.

A You didn't finish yet?

B I'm going to finish it tonight.

A How much do you still have to do?

B I'm going to start it tonight.

A You haven't even started yet? It's six pages.

B It's all right. Some of us are going to stay up and pull an all-nighter on this. Get it done.

A Really?

B We're gonna start our papers, write our papers, and finish our papers tonight.

A Wow.

B Wanna come over and help?

A No! I don't want to stay up all night.

B C'mon. We're all gonna write our papers, and then proof each other's papers.

A No thanks.

B It'll be fun.

A No fun. Mine's done.

B Very funny. Ha. Ha.

A I wish you told me earlier. I would have helped you get started on this. Why did you wait 'til the last minute? You could have asked me.

B Thanks. I didn't think of it.

A Why not?

B I don't know. I guess sometimes ... I have trouble asking for help.

A I think a lot of people do.

B Really?

A Yeah. Goes with the territory.

B What territory?

A Human being territory.

B That's a pretty big territory.

A Yeah. Sorry you have to deal with this. Can you ask for an extension?

B No. I just want to get it done now. I got myself into this and -

A Yeah, I understand.

B Sure you don't want to come over? We'll have pizza.

A I don't wanna eat pizza at four in the morning. I wanna sleep at four in the morning.

B Yeah. Me too.

A Tell you what. I'll get up an hour early for school and proof your paper for you. That way you have someone with a fresh eye looking it over.

B Thanks.

A That's how we roll.

B Okay. I'll save you some pizza.

A Is that a promise or a threat?

B Cold pizza? Breakfast of champions!

The School Newspaper

A Hey, you got a minute?

B Sure. What's up?

A Can I interview you?

B Interview me for what?

A School paper. I just started writing for them today.

B Hey, that's great. Congratulations. What are you writing about?

A I don't know. They told me to interview somebody for my first story.

B Yeah, but you need a topic, a subject.

A I know, I know. Any ideas?

B Uh … I think you're supposed to come up with the story idea.

A Yeah, I've been thinking, but it hasn't hit me yet.

B How do the other writers do it?

A They didn't tell me. They skipped over that part.

B How about a story on how to come up with ideas for stories?

A That's kinda funny.

B I'm kinda serious. If you're having trouble with this, then other people must be too.

A Probably so. Makes sense.

B Lots of people have to come up with ideas to write about. Not just for their school paper, but English class, college essays, all kinds of stuff.

A So where do I start?

B I'm not sure. I think my uncle was talking about something like this.

A Which uncle? The one I met?

B Yeah. The nice one, not the crazy one. My Uncle Matt.

A Does he work for a newspaper?

B No, but he writes stuff for Toastmasters.

A What's Toastmasters?

B This group he belongs to. They practice getting up and speaking in front of people.

A Speaking about what?

B Anything, whatever they want. They get together and make speeches 'cause a lot of people are scared to talk in public. He took me once when I was little. I thought it would be boring, but it was actually pretty cool.

A What's that have to do with the school paper?

B They have to write the speeches. He needs something to speak about, but first he has to write it.

A Oh, now I get it. So what does he do? How does he do it?

B   He says ideas for speeches are everywhere, all around us, and we just have to pull the good ones out of the air. There's plenty to go around.

A   But how does he find good ones?

B   All kinds of ways. Sometimes he goes through a magazine. He says he'll find four or five articles that are interesting enough to write a speech about. Maybe you can try that.

A   Find something in the magazine that kids at school could relate to?

B   Something or *somebody*.

A   What do you mean?

B   Maybe there's a celebrity or a famous athlete everyone wants to read about. Or you can ask kids from our sports teams how they got started.

A   That's really good. Maybe I can ask our football team about the NFL.

B   Yeah, you could tie that together. Even interview the coach.

A   That's another good idea! Ask our coach what he thinks about the pro coaches.

B   See? Uncle Matt's right. Ideas are everywhere.

Trying, Trying Tryouts

A Back so soon?

B Apparently.

A How'd the tryout go?

B Well...I thought it went fine. Unfortunately, Coach... did not agree.

A You're kidding!

B No.

A How is that even possible? You're just about the best athlete in our school.

B I don't know. New sport for me, I guess. Maybe it's just not my game.

A What exactly happened?

B He put us all through some drills. Then he called out a few of us and told us we could go home. The rest were invited to stay longer and work out with the team.

A Did he tell you to come back?

B Yeah, next year. He said I can try again next year.

A You have to wait a whole year?

B Yeah, 'till next season.

A Don't get discouraged. Even Muhammad Ali lost a few times, and he was supposed to be the best boxer ever.

B Maybe I can get Muhammad Ali to punch out that idiot Coach.

A C'mon, don't be like that.

B It's aggravating, that's all.

A You know the old saying – you can't win 'em all.

B I just really expected to make the team, okay? Not only make it, but I thought I was going to be one of the star players. And now I don't even make the first cut. I feel like a total loser.

A If at first you don't succeed …

B You know, for a teenager you have a lot of old sayings.

A There's a lot of truth in those old sayings.

B I guess.

A I read somewhere that Michael Jordan didn't even make his high school basketball team the first time he tried out.

B Michael Jordan didn't make his high school team? Air Jordan?

A Not the first time. Then he worked hard, applied himself …

B And made history.

A Got a funny feeling he didn't waste much time complaining.

B Got a funny feeling I shouldn't, either.

A Probably not. What are you gonna do instead?

B Train ten times harder. Get myself ready for next year.

A Yeah, that sounds like a good idea.

B Yeah, I think so too.

The Waiting Game

A Any word?

B Not yet.

A No news is good news.

B I guess. It's nerve wracking, though.

A Gotta think positive. No reason you shouldn't get this.

B Don't be so sure. There's so much competition. So many kids would like to do this.

A Don't worry about them. Just worry about you.

B But we *have to* think about who we're up against. We *have to* worry about the competition.

A You know what my dad says? If we work hard, do our best, and stay focused ... we won't *have* any competition.

B Yeah, yeah, yeah. That sounds good, but I still think about how many other kids might be better qualified.

A Don't be so sure.

B That's just where my head goes. That's the way my mind works.

A I read those recommendation letters you submitted. You sound pretty qualified for this thing.

B It's just been making me nervous. This is the kind of internship that would look really good on my college applications.

A So what?

B So it's even more reason to be nervous about it.

A I think it's just the opposite. More reason to be calm and confident and excited about it.

B Yeah, yeah, yeah. I wish I could.

A You can. What's easy to do is also easy not to do.

B What's that supposed to mean?

A Think about it logically. Think about anything we do that's not good for us.

B That's easy. I do that every day.

A It's just as easy to do the opposite — something that's good.

B I'm not getting this. You're talking in circles.

A Listen, it's easy to sit home on the couch, eat ice cream, and be lazy.

B I know!

A But it's just as easy to get up and go for a run, get up and go to the library, get up and meet a friend.

B You're telling me I need more "get up and go?"

A It's the same with worry. It's easy to worry. It's too easy. But it's just as easy to get your mind right, think positive, and make a decision to have a good attitude.

B But I don't know for sure that –

A You're going to get this internship. This is yours.

B How do you know what –

A This is yours.

Did You Ever Wonder?

A Can I ask you something?

B You just did.

A Come on. I'm serious.

B Okay, okay. Ask away.

A Did you ever wonder where we all came from?

B What do you mean? Where who came from?

A Everyone. Everything. People, animals, plants, flowers, the world, the stars, the universe. Just everything.

B Not really. I try not to.

A I wonder about that stuff all the time.

B Why?

A I don't know. I don't know what to believe in sometimes.

B Well … are you talking about religion?

A No, not exactly. Even people who believe in a Creator don't agree on everything.

B I still don't understand what you're talking about.

A Well, I have one side of my family that's Christian, and the other side is Jewish.

B So what?

A They both believe in a higher power, but they don't agree on everything.

B Well, I think I know what you mean. But nobody's going to have all the answers.

A I guess not.

B Of course not. My little brother still thinks the stork brought him. Meanwhile, my grandpa keeps saying he's ready to see *his* mom and dad in Heaven any time now. Nobody really knows.

A What about atheists? They say it's the Big Bang Theory.

B They don't have all the answers, either. That's why it's called a theory, not a fact.

A How about evolution?

B Okay. The way I see it … if we all descended from monkeys …

A Yeah …

B … then why do we still have monkeys?

A Good point. So what do we do?

B I guess we just do our best.

A Treat everyone the way we'd like to be treated?

B Exactly. I think that's the whole secret to everything. Just be a good person.

A That's pretty simple and straightforward when you think about it.

B Sure. Good advice for everyone, Christians, Jews, atheists.

A Even monkeys.

B Especially monkeys.

A I know. Monkeys are annoying, right?

B Tell me about it.

A Always screaming … jumping around …

B Eating all the bananas.

A That's pretty funny.

B Hey, we gotta have a few laughs, right?

Study Group

A   I think we should start a study group.

B   What do you mean?

A   You never heard of a study group?

B   Sure. I've heard the expression, but I was never in one before.

A   Me neither.

B   I never knew exactly what it is ... how it works ...

A   I think a lot of people don't.

B   So what's the point?

A   There's probably things kids at school wanna work on. That's the point.

B   If nobody even knows what a study group does - then why should we start one?

A   To figure it out. To help each other.

B   I don't want to start a group just to have something to belong to. That would be a total waste of time.

A   No. We'd start it with a purpose.

B   Example.

A   Take you and me, for example. What classes do we have that are too hard?

B   Definitely history.

A   Definitely. Anything else?

B   Maybe English.

A That's what I was thinking. But I thought you were having an easier time with English this year.

B Ah … I don't know. It's easier than last year, but I could still be doing better.

A Okay, let's figure this out. What's easier about your English class this year? What specifically is easier?

B I think the teacher's better. She's not as boring.

A Good. Anything else?

B The books we have to read are more interesting. I actually want to read these.

A So what do you need to work on?

B Probably my writing. The essays on the books and the stories we read.

A Book reports?

B Yeah.

A See, I'm pretty good with that. Grammar, sentence structure.

B That's what I always struggle with. I have an easy time coming up with ideas for papers, but a hard time writing them.

A Because of all the little detail stuff.

B Exactly. The detail stuff.

A I can help you with grammar and spelling if you can help me find ideas to write about. I have a hard time finding the right way to start. The big picture.

B Well, I can definitely help you come up with topics. Interesting topics too. That part's easy for me.

A And I can help you proofread, edit, and make corrections.

B This sounds good. There should be other kids that are interested too.

A I think that's how a study group works.

B We benefit from each other's strong points.

A But let's make sure — when we get together to study — that we don't just joke around and waste time.

B Yeah. I already told you. I don't wanna do it just to have a group to belong to.

A Cool.

B Way cool.

Tutor

A Are you going to sports camp this summer?

B I'd like to, but I don't think I'll be able to make it.

A Why not?

B Looks like I might have to go to summer school instead.

A Why? Are you trying to graduate early?

B Yeah, right. I wish! I'll be lucky if I don't flunk out.

A Flunk out? Flunk out of school?

B Yeah. I'm failing two classes — math and science. Got a 50 on my mid- term.

A Ouch.

B Yeah. Double ouch.

A Have you talked to your teachers about it?

B What am I gonna say? What are they gonna tell me? My grades are low, and they're supposed to be high?

A You know, you're not the first kid to have this problem.

B Thank you for clearing that up. I kinda thought I invented it.

A C'mon, I'm serious.

B I'm serious too. I'm flunking two classes. What do you want me to say – I'm not flunking 'em?

A What I'm trying to say is that there's plenty of kids to have this problem before you, plenty of kids have solved this problem before you, and plenty of kids will solve this problem after you. So there's always a way out of it, a way around it, or a way through it.

B Okay, Einstein. How?

A I don't know. Have you thought about getting a tutor?

B No!

A Why not?

B It's embarrassing! I don't want everybody to think I'm some dumb kid that needs help tying his shoes.

A Who's everybody?

B Everybody at school. They'll make fun of me. They'll say I'm dumb.

A What do you care what people think? Know what my dad says? "Don't worry about what people think. They don't do it very often."

B That's funny, but I'm not changing my mind. You're not talking me into this.

A Look, the important thing is that a tutor can help you pass these two classes that are giving you trouble.

B You're not talking me into this.

A Would you rather be talked in or flunked out?

B Tutors are for idiots.

A I had a tutor last year for English. Helped me a lot.

B English? English is easy, my easiest subject. You were flunking English?

A No, I wasn't exactly flunking.

B So why did you need a tutor?

A My tutor helped me go from a C to a B plus.

B That's pretty good. That's a big jump.

A To tell you the truth, I still work with the tutor. Just once a month now to keep me on track.

B Isn't it kind of expensive? Right now … I'm not sure my parents can do it.

A I think there's all kinds of tutors. There are definitely some real expensive ones. I found my tutor at the library. It's free.

B Free? How can it be free?

A I think it's through a volunteer organization. Just a group of really nice people who want to give back and help people.

B The library on Oak Street?

A Yeah, they're great. I love that place.

B Do you think they have someone for science and math?

A I bet you they do. If they don't, they'll know where you can find somebody.

B Well … would you mind going over there with me?

A Sure. I'll introduce you to the librarian.

B Thank you very much. I really appreciate it. Maybe if it worked for you, it'll work for me.

Rehab

A Are you friends with Laurie?

B Laurie from science class?

A No, not her. Oh ... I don't know her last name. Pretty. Brunette.

B The new girl? The one who runs track?

A Yeah, yeah, yeah, that's her.

B I know her, but not too well. She takes my bus.

A I don't know her too well, either. Did you hear about her sister?

B No, what about her sister?

A Well ... I heard her sister was in pretty bad shape.

B Oh, no. Did she have an accident?

A No, not exactly. She had to get checked into rehab.

B What? Are you serious?

A Totally serious.

B She's so young. I met her once. She's in college, right?

A She *was* away at college. Now she's here in rehab.

B What year was she?

A She's a freshman. She just started college.

B What happened to her?

A I don't know exactly. I think she got in with some kind of a bad crowd at school. Her roommate and the roommate's boyfriend, from what I heard.

B Is it just alcohol or …

A No, I don't think it's alcohol. It's drugs.

B Wow. Wow. What … uh, what kind of drugs?

A Not sure.

B I don't want to gossip, but … does anyone else in her family … I mean …

A No … no, I don't think anyone else in her family has a problem with any of that stuff.

B Not the parents or anyone?

A No, I heard they're all pretty clean, pretty straight-laced.

B Not even drinking? No drinking problems?

A Maybe … New Year's Eve … or once in a while … but I'm pretty sure there's no issue at all with that.

B Seemed like such a nice girl. She was so pretty.

A Stop! Don't say "seemed." Don't say "was." Don't talk about her in the past tense. It's not cool.

B Sorry.

A It's okay.

B I wonder if they need anything. The family, Laurie.

A Maybe we can do something for them?

B Yeah. Laurie hasn't made too many friends yet.

A She can probably use a couple right now. Friends who stick by her.

B Just help her with stuff. Bring her homework if she misses a day.

A Take her out for a burger.

B Do you think we can go visit her sister in … the place?

A I don't know if they allow visitors.

B I don't either. So maybe we'll do something else.

A Like what?

B Visit Laurie, bring her a little gift. Let her know we're thinking of her, hoping everything turns out okay.

A Really good idea. Maybe we'll get one of those big, giant cards. Everyone can sign it.

B I don't know if we should tell everyone. Maybe Laurie and her family are private? Maybe … it's not our place?

A If we just tell people she's having a tough time right now, get everyone to sign the card …

B Yeah, I think that would be good.

A Me too. I want to do something, but it's hard to know the right thing.

B But that's why people do nothing. We gotta try. We have to do what we can for this girl.

Saturday Morning

A Do you want to come see him?

B Yeah, I do. What time are you doing it?

A My dad wants to do it first thing in the morning. Get it over with.

B What time?

A He said about nine. Then he wants to take us all out for breakfast someplace nice. Waffles and omelettes and stuff.

B I don't know if I'm going to feel much like eating, though.

A Yeah, I know. But my dad says we should try to do something nice if we have to do something sad.

B Well ... that is a nice idea, I guess.

A Yeah. He always has really good ideas like that. Kinda old-fashioned, but really very nice too.

B How about your mom? She gonna be okay with all this?

A No, not really. She said she just can't. She's really been crying a lot.

B I can imagine.

A She had him from a kitten. Since she was in college.

B I can't even imagine your mom in college.

A She has this whole big photo album of pictures with that little cat. She was so attached to him.

B It's weird, the way he used to follow her around.

A Like a dog.

B Yeah, he was just like a dog.

A More like a dog than a cat. Everybody used to say so.

B Well, your mom took really good care of him. Not that many kitties get to live as long as he did.

A That's what we've all been telling her.

B Yeah, your mom is awesome.

A She's definitely awesome.

B I hope she starts to feel better soon.

A Thanks. It's just gonna take her some time, I guess. I'll tell her you said hello.

B Good. I'll see you tomorrow morning.

A Remember to save room for waffles.

B Yeah, waffles will be good.

Is This Bullying?

A Hey, can I ask your advice on something?

B Sure. What's up?

A I got into it with my mom last night. She thinks I was a little out of line.

B What happened?

A We were watching this show on TV, one of those talent shows, and I said that the singer was fat. I didn't mean anything by it, but my mom thought it was rude.

B Well, it depends on how you said it, I guess. I think it's a tricky thing.

A I wasn't trying to insult the girl or anything. But she was definitely a little on the heavy side. I was just describing the way she looked.

B Yeah, but I can see how somebody would take it the wrong way.

A My mom took it the wrong way. She said it's bullying. How could it be bullying if I don't even see the girl in person? We're not even in the same room.

B Maybe your mom is thinking of cyber bullying, like on the Internet. I guess on TV it could be almost the same thing.

A But I didn't mean it that way.

B Maybe not, but it could still be pretty hurtful to somebody.

A I guess.

B Remember that girl on the news that killed herself because everybody was posting that she was ugly?

A I think so. There were a couple of stories like that. There was that other one where the boyfriend said he hated her.

B It's awful. Some people take things very hard, so we have to be extra careful about what we say in public. Think about her poor parents, her brothers and sisters.

A I guess I never thought about it that much.

B Like if this singer is a little heavier, maybe there's a reason.

A Like what?

B I don't know. Maybe a medical reason. Maybe she's depressed and she eats to feel better.

A You mean like bingeing and then dieting?

B Maybe. Maybe she has a slow metabolism. I don't know. I didn't see the girl.

A Well … I guess it could be any one of those things. But honestly, I was just trying to describe her.

B How was her singing?

A It was really good. She had a beautiful voice.

B Why don't you describe her that way? She's the girl with the beautiful voice.

A Yeah. You're right. You're absolutely right. That's a much better way to describe her.

B   Maybe your mom is just trying to tell you that if we can't say something nice about somebody … we shouldn't say anything at all.

A   Pretty good advice.

B   And it's always good to give someone a compliment when we can.

A   That's one way to keep out of trouble. Sure can't hurt.

B   Yeah … can't hurt anyone else that way, either.

Can I Borrow?

A Hey. Can I borrow your car?

B No!

A What?! Why not?!

B Because!

A "Because?" What do you mean, "Because?"

B Because my parents say I'm not supposed to lend my car to anyone.

A That's ridiculous.

B It's not ridiculous. That's their rule. That's it.

A Don't be such a baby! Do you always do everything your mom and dad tell you – like a little kid?

B Nice try. My parents pay for this car every month, and they want me to be the only driver. I'm not supposed to give it to anyone.

A Wow! Why do they have to be so strict with you? It's definitely not cool.

B They pay for it, and they have the right to make the rules about who drives it. That's it. Done.

A I don't know why you have to be so rude. I thought you were my friend.

B *I'm* being rude?

A Very rude. Extremely rude. Your parents sound really strict too. Strict and super rude.

B Somebody in this conversation's being rude. But it's not me, and it's definitely not my parents.

A You mean me?!

B If the shoe fits ...

A What does that mean?

B It's a famous expression. If the shoe fits, wear it.

A That's not a famous expression. I've never heard it before.

B "If the shoe fits" is a very famous expression.

A I think it's stupid. Did your parents tell you that too?

B As a matter of fact, they did.

A So you're telling me you're not going to let me borrow your car?

B Right.

A So that's it? That's your final answer?

B Yes.

A I can't borrow your car?

B No.

A Because the shoe fits?

B Yes.

A Can I borrow your shoes?

B No.

A Why not?

B I need them to drive my car.

I Don't Drink

A Want to grab a six-pack with me?

B What?!

A Beers. You know, brews. Couple of cold ones.

B No. I don't drink.

A Why not?

B We're not supposed to. It's against the law.

A Come on.

B Come on? You come on. We're underage.

A So? What's the big deal? Everybody does it.

B Everybody doesn't do it. Kids don't do it. We're in high
   school. We're minors.

A Relax. What's wrong with you today?

B What's wrong with me? We're not allowed to drink. It's
   illegal. What's wrong with me? What's wrong with you?!

A Give it a rest. I'm just trying to unwind and have a little
   fun. That's what you should do too. You're too tense.

B I'm not tense at all. I'm rational, logical, and I follow the
   law.

A Come on. School's almost over. This is supposed to be a
   time for all of us to celebrate.

B Good. Get yourself a nice, cold milk shake.

A Very funny. Ha. Ha.

B Have a milk shake and celebrate how you won't be getting a DUI tonight.

A You sound like my mother.

B Good.

A What do you mean "good?"

B Hope you appreciate her more than you appreciate me!

A Okay, now what's *that* supposed to mean?

B It means you should be grateful to have a mom who's concerned for your safety and welfare. A lot of kids don't, you know.

A Where do you come up with this weird stuff?

B From *my* mom, who's concerned with *my* safety and welfare.

President Number Twenty

A You okay? You look a little funny.

B Yeah. Just been thinking a lot.

A Stay out of your head. It's a very bad neighborhood.

B I'm serious. I was reading in our history book about President Garfield.

A Garfield? Never heard of him.

B He was President a long time ago. I think he was friends with Abraham Lincoln. Way, way back.

A Was that on our syllabus? I don't remember seeing anything about him. Did we have a homework assignment?

B No. I was just reading another chapter on my own. It wasn't assigned, but I thought it was interesting.

A Now you're starting to scare me.

B There was this article about the Presidents who were assassinated. And they also talked about the Presidents that were shot — or shot at — and then survived.

A What happened to Garfield?

B He was assassinated. Somebody shot him in the back.

A They shot him in the back?!

B Yeah, but then the worst part was he didn't even die right away. He lived for three months in all this pain while the doctors tried to save him.

A Why couldn't they save him? He was the President.

B Because it was such a long time ago. They didn't even have the x-ray machine yet. His doctors couldn't find the bullet.

A You're kidding me.

B No.

A That's awful.

B They kept doing all these surgeries on him, and they kept making him worse.

A How could the surgeries make him worse?

B The doctors didn't even know about germs yet. They didn't wash their hands. They didn't wear gloves. They didn't scrub up or anything.

A Sounds really primitive. When was all this? How long ago?

B Not too long after Abraham Lincoln was shot. A little while after the Civil War.

A How come we don't learn about Garfield in school?

B I don't know. I guess nobody thinks he's important enough.

A How long was he President?

B Not very long. He got shot three or four months after he took office. Then he lived another three months with the bullet in his back. Then he died.

A I think this is just a horrible, horrible story.

B I know. It's been running through my mind since I first read about it. It really makes you think.

A It's just … I don't know … it's just so sad.

B It makes you think about how much we have to be grateful for nowadays. About how much doctors can do today compared to a hundred years ago.

A And just an x-ray could have saved him … something so simple.

B It's simple now. Not back then.

A Yeah, I guess so. What was his first name, anyway?

B James. James Garfield.

A President James Garfield.

B And nobody even knows about him.

About the Author

Photo by Greg James

Mike Kimmel is a film, television, stage, and commercial actor and acting coach. He is a twenty-plus year member of SAG-AFTRA with extensive experience in both the New York and Los Angeles markets. He has worked with directors Francis Ford Coppola, Robert Townsend, and Christopher Cain. TV credits include *Game of Silence, Zoo, Treme, In Plain Sight, Cold Case, Breakout Kings, Memphis Beat,* and *Buffy the Vampire Slayer.* He was a regular sketch comedy player on *The Tonight Show,* performing live on stage and in pre-taped segments with Jay Leno for eleven years.

Mike has appeared in dozens of theatrical plays on both coasts, including Radio City Music Hall, Equity Library Theater, Stella Adler Theater, and Theater at the Improv. He trained with Michael Shurtleff, William Hickey, Ralph Marrero, Gloria Maddox, Harold Sylvester, Wendy Davis, Amy Hunter, Bob Collier, and Stuart Robinson. He has a B.A. from Brandeis University and an M.A. from California State University.

As an educator and lecturer, he has taught at Upper Iowa University, University of New Orleans, University of Phoenix, and in both the Los Angeles and Beverly Hills School Districts. He is a two-time past president of New Orleans Toastmasters, the public speaking organization, and often serves as a speech contest judge. Mike has written and collaborated on numerous scripts for stage and screen. His full-length historical drama on Presidents Lincoln and Garfield was a 2013 semi-finalist in the National Playwrights Conference at the Eugene O'Neill Theater Center. He is the 2014 recipient of the Excellence in Teaching Award from Upper Iowa University.